# A walk in the
# Village

Written by Sally Hewitt
Photography by Chris Fairclough

# W
## FRANKLIN WATTS
LONDON · SYDNEY

First published in 2005 by
Franklin Watts
96 Leonard Street
London EC2A 4XD

Franklin Watts Australia
45-51 Huntley Street
Alexandria NSW 2015

© Franklin Watts 2005

Editors: Caryn Jenner, Sarah Ridley
Designer: Louise Best
Art director: Jonathan Hair
Photography: Chris Fairclough
Map: Hardlines

Many thanks to Mark, Philippa and Sophie
Campbell for agreeing to appear in the book.

A CIP catalogue record for this book is available
from the British Library

ISBN 0 7496 6043 0

Dewey decimal classification number: 307.72

Printed in China

# Contents

# The village

This old village is surrounded by fields and hills. You can see the church tower from all around the village.

A sign welcomes you to the village.

# New and old

New houses are around the edge of the village and old houses in the middle.

The old
houses are
built with
chalk rock,
flint and brick.

# Village school

The old school house is too small for all the village children now. They go to school in the new building next door.

How do you think the new school is different from the old school?

# The church

The old church overlooks the village green. How can you tell that the church was not all built at the same time?

The names on the old gravestones are wearing away.

Wedding flowers decorate the church doorway.

# The village green

You can walk along an old cobblestone road. The new road is made of tarmac.

The market cross stands on the
green where the village market
used to be held. What do you
think was sold at the market?

# The village pond

The pond in the village square
is surrounded by grass and trees.

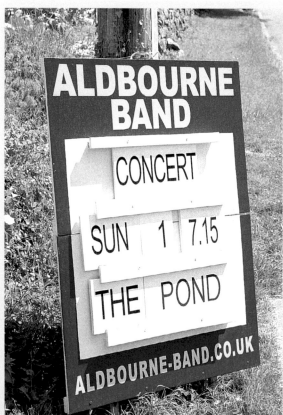

In the summer, the band gives open-air concerts next to the pond.

# The pump

Water still pours from the old pump. In the past, horses drank the water when they were passing.

Roads from all directions meet by the pump. Why is this a good place for a bus stop?

# General store

You can post letters and buy everything you need at the general store.

A mounting block stands outside. It was used to climb up onto a horse.

# The farm

A tractor drives
through the village.

The farm is on the edge of
the village. Why is the farm
gate so wide?

# Farm buildings

There are horses in the field behind the big farm buildings.

The old grain store stands on staddles to keep out rats.

staddle

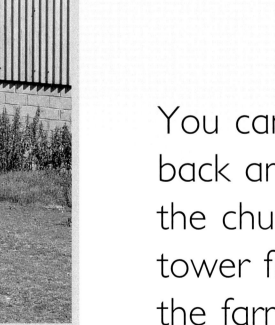

You can look back and see the church tower from the farm.

# Map

You can start a walk from any point on a map. To follow the walk in this book, put your finger on **Start** and trace the route.

# Key

house

school

church

green

pub

market cross

pond

pump

general store

farm

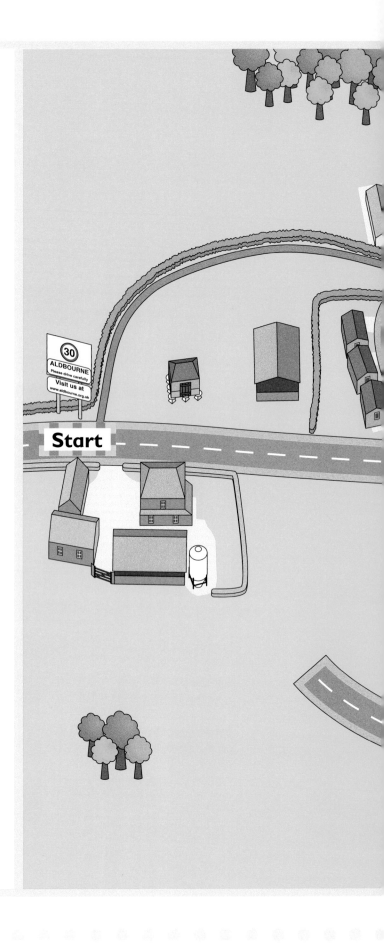

# Quiz

A city has skyscrapers and tall buildings. What is the tallest building in the village?

*Look at pages 7, 8, 12 and 25.*

Old and new houses are built with brick. What else was used to build the old houses?

*Look at page 9.*

Sunday services are held at the village church. What kind of service is often held on Saturdays?

*Look at page 13.*

The green is in the middle of the village. Can you remember what stands in the middle of the village green?

*Look at page 15.*

Today, people arrive at the village by bus and car. How did they travel long ago?

*Look at page 18.*

Today, modern farm buildings protect the grain. How did staddles protect the grain in the past?

*Look at page 25.*

# Index